Mapping
MOUNTAINS

Robert Walker

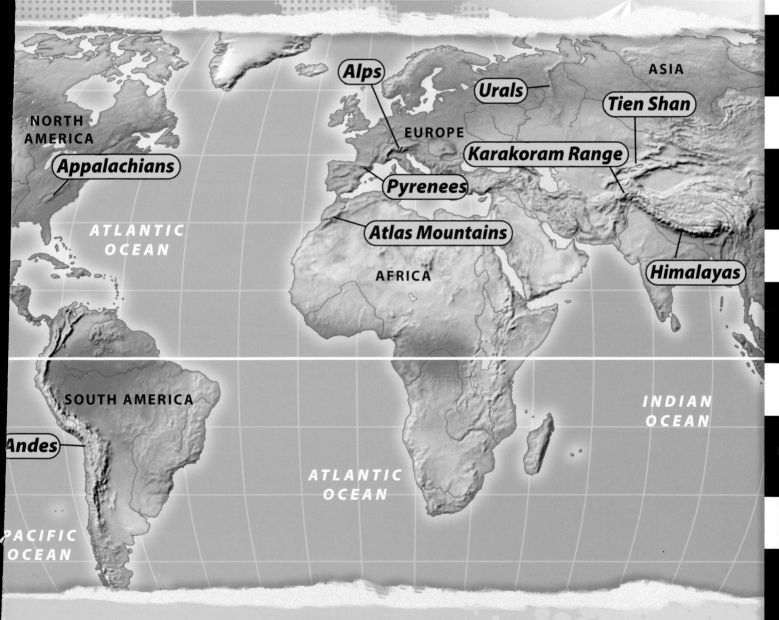

ASIA

Alps

Urals

Tien Shan

NORTH
AMERICA

EUROPE

Karakoram Range

Appalachians

Pyrenees

ATLANTIC
OCEAN

Atlas Mountains

Himalayas

AFRICA

SOUTH AMERICA

INDIAN
OCEAN

Andes

ATLANTIC
OCEAN

PACIFIC
OCEAN

 **Marshall Cavendish**
Benchmark
New York

This edition first published in 2011 in the United States
by Marshall Cavendish Benchmark.

Marshall Cavendish Benchmark
99 White Plains Road
Tarrytown, NY 10591
www.marshallcavendish.us

Published by Marshall Cavendish Benchmark
An imprint of Marshall Cavendish Corporation

Other Marshall Cavendish Offices:
Marshall Cavendish International (Asia) Private Limited, 1 New Industrial Road, Singapore 536196 • Marshall Cavendish
International (Thailand) Co Ltd. 253 Asoke, 12th Flr, Sukhumvit 21 Road, Klongtoey Nua, Wattana, Bangkok 10110,
Thailand • Marshall Cavendish (Malaysia) Sdn Bhd, Times Subang, Lot 46, Subang Hi-Tech Industrial Park,
Batu Tiga, 40000 Shah Alam, Selangor Darul Ehsan, Malaysia

Marshall Cavendish is a trademark of Times Publishing Limited

Library of Congress Cataloging-in-Publication Data
Walker, Robert.
Mapping mountains.
p. cm. — (Mapping our world)
Includes bibliographical references and index.
Summary: "Introduces maps and teaches essential mapping skills, including how to create,
use, and interpret maps of mountains"—Provided by publisher.
ISBN 978-1-60870-116-2
1. Mountain mapping. 2. Atlases. I. Title.
G1021.W16 2011
526.0914'3—dc22
2010001562

Created by Q2AMedia
Series Editor: Deborah Rogus
Art Director: Harleen Mehta
Client Service Manager: Santosh Vasudevan
Project Manager: Kumar Kunal
Line Artist: Vinay Kumar
Coloring Artist: Subhash Vohra
Photo research: Ekta Sharma, Rajeev Parmar

The photographs in this book are used by permission and through the courtesy of:

Cover: NASA
Half title: Joe LeMonnier

4-5: Danny Warren/Shutterstock; 5t: Joe LeMonnier; 5b: Holger Mette/Istockphoto; 6: Joe LeMonnier; 7: Joe LeMonnier;
8-9: Joe LeMonnier; 10: U.S. Geological Survey; 12: Craig Hansen/Istockphoto; 14t: Joe LeMonnier; 17t: Stacey Tighe,
University of Rhode Island/USGS; 17b: Joe LeMonnier; 18t: Joe LeMonnier; 18b: Bettmann/Corbis; 20: Joe LeMonnier;
21t: Lee Prince/Shutterstock; 21b: Karen Kasmauski/Corbis; 22: Andrea Pistolesi/Photolibrary; 23t: Joe LeMonnier;
23b: Joe LeMonnier; 24: David Muench/Corbis; 25t: Joe LeMonnier; 25b: WA State Historical Society/AP Images;
26: Ilja Masik/Shutterstock; 27: Guenter Guni/Istockphoto; 28: Amaia Eta Gotzon; 29: Martin Hladky/Shutterstock

Q2AMedia Art Bank: 11, 12, 13, 14, 15, 16, 19

Printed in Malaysia

135642

Contents

Words in **bold** are defined in the Glossary.

Earth's Giants

Challenging, amazing, dangerous, massive, breathtaking—there aren't enough words to describe the majesty of mountains. They are Earth's giants, towering above the land and stretching hundreds—even thousands—of miles across Earth's surface.

Why Map Mountains?

Mountains are more than just impressive. They're also important. We map mountains because they affect how we live, where we go, and how we play. Maps help us understand Earth's history, plan for the future, keep people safe, and find **natural resources** like fresh water, **minerals**, **metals**, and timber.

Mountains have fascinated people for centuries. Hundreds of people have spent their lives trying to conquer them, map them, and study them.

Did You Know?

Mountains cover one-fifth of the Earth and are home to almost one-tenth of the world's population.

Mount Everest

At 29,035 feet (8,850 meters), Mount Everest is the highest peak in the world. It's part of the Himalayan mountain range that is located between Tibet and Nepal.

During the nineteenth century, teams from Britain began mapping the mountain. Unfortunately, these mapping teams couldn't actually climb Everest. They had to measure and map it from miles away.

These maps weren't very accurate, but they helped future explorers climb Everest. Everest was finally conquered in 1953, when Sir Edmund Hillary reached the **summit**.

CHINA

Mt. Everest

Tibet

NEPAL

INDIA

Did You Know?

People who live in Nepal and Tibet don't call it Mount Everest. In Nepal it's called *Sagarmatha* (goddess of the sky), and in Tibet it's called *Chomolungma* (mother goddess of the universe).

Reading Maps

Maps can provide information about Earth's land and water features. For example, maps of mountains can show elevation, natural resources, and routes.

Using Map Tools

Even though there are many different types of maps, most maps have certain elements, or features, in common. By learning to use these features, you can read almost any map.

LINES OF LONGITUDE
These vertical lines, also called meridians, run north to south and measure the distance east and west of the prime meridian. Lines of longitude are measured in degrees. The prime meridian is 0° and meridians measure up to 180° east or west.

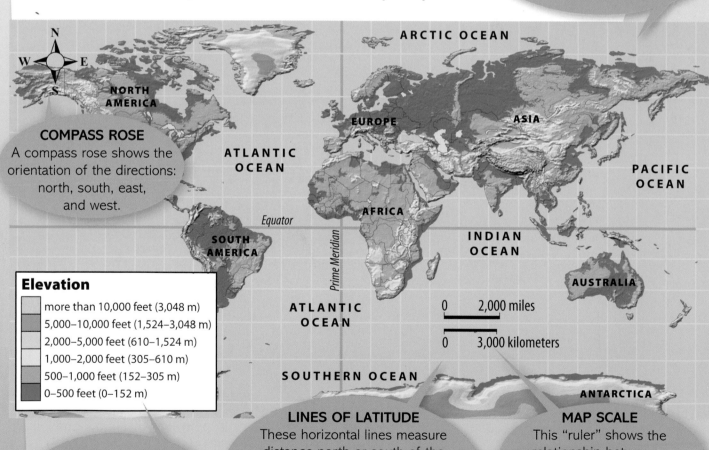

ARCTIC OCEAN

NORTH AMERICA

EUROPE

ASIA

COMPASS ROSE
A compass rose shows the orientation of the directions: north, south, east, and west.

ATLANTIC OCEAN

PACIFIC OCEAN

Equator

AFRICA

SOUTH AMERICA

INDIAN OCEAN

Prime Meridian

AUSTRALIA

Elevation

	more than 10,000 feet (3,048 m)
	5,000–10,000 feet (1,524–3,048 m)
	2,000–5,000 feet (610–1,524 m)
	1,000–2,000 feet (305–610 m)
	500–1,000 feet (152–305 m)
	0–500 feet (0–152 m)

ATLANTIC OCEAN

0   2,000 miles

0   3,000 kilometers

SOUTHERN OCEAN

ANTARCTICA

KEY or LEGEND
The key explains the colors or symbols that are used on the map.

LINES OF LATITUDE
These horizontal lines measure distance north or south of the equator. The equator circles Earth halfway between the North and South poles. Lines of latitude are measured in degrees (°). The equator is 0° and the poles are 90°.

MAP SCALE
This "ruler" shows the relationship between a certain distance on a map and the actual distance on Earth.

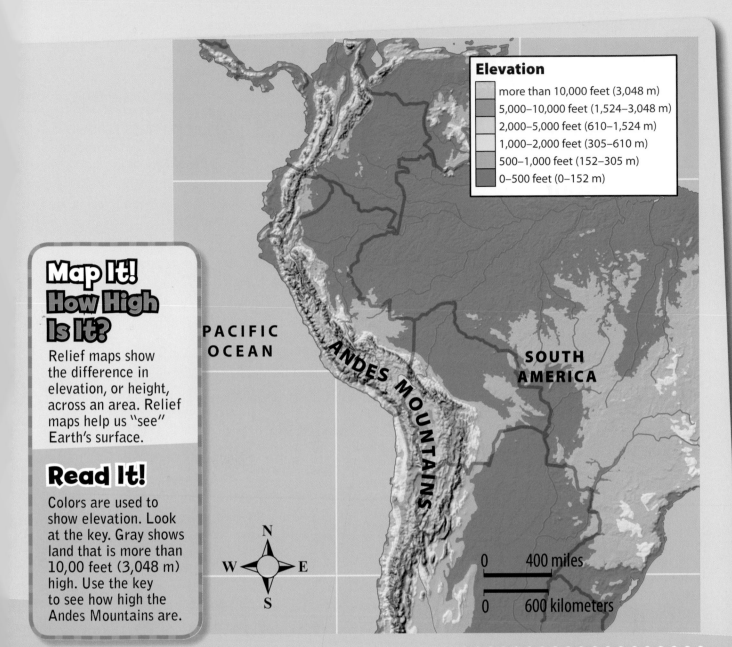

Elevation

- more than 10,000 feet (3,048 m)
- 5,000–10,000 feet (1,524–3,048 m)
- 2,000–5,000 feet (610–1,524 m)
- 1,000–2,000 feet (305–610 m)
- 500–1,000 feet (152–305 m)
- 0–500 feet (0–152 m)

PACIFIC OCEAN

ANDES MOUNTAINS

SOUTH AMERICA

N
W E
S

| 0 | 400 miles |
| 0 | 600 kilometers |

Map It! How High Is It?

Relief maps show the difference in elevation, or height, across an area. Relief maps help us "see" Earth's surface.

Read It!

Colors are used to show elevation. Look at the key. Gray shows land that is more than 10,00 feet (3,048 m) high. Use the key to see how high the Andes Mountains are.

What Maps Can We Use?

We can use several types of maps to study mountains. To show elevation and land features, we use topographic maps and relief maps. Some relief maps are even three-dimensional (3-D). Thematic maps are used to display a specific type of information, such as natural resources, political boundaries, or vegetation.

Mapping from Space

Mapmakers use the latest technologies to map mountains. **Satellites** take detailed images of mountains from space. **GPS** (global positioning system) may be used to track and mark places on Earth's surface and to provide exact locations. Once the data has been collected, **GIS** (geographic information system) technology is used to create maps and 3-D images.

Ranges of the World

Mountain ranges are long chains of mountains. Ranges can divide continents, block out the horizon, and affect the weather. Some are thick with trees, while others are cold, windy wastelands.

The All-Time Greats

Some ranges are known around the world for their beauty, their dangers, or their history. They show up in novels, movies, and travelogues. Here are ten of the best known.

The **PYRENEES MOUNTAINS** are located on the border separating France and Spain. The range's highest point, Pico de Aneto, is 11,168 feet (3,404 m) high.

NORTH AMERICA

Rockies

Appalachians

PACIFIC OCEAN

ATLANTIC OCEAN

The **APPALACHIANS** have some of the world's oldest peaks. One section, called the Smokies, is blanketed in a smokelike haze caused by changes in temperature.

The **ROCKY MOUNTAINS** run from northern Canada to the United States' border with Mexico. The highest peak is Mount Elbert, at 14,433 feet (4,399 m).

equator

SOUTH AMERICA

Andes

PACIFIC OCEAN

The **ANDES** in South America are the longest mountain range in the world, stretching 5,000 miles (8,050 kilometers) across seven countries.

ANTARCTICA

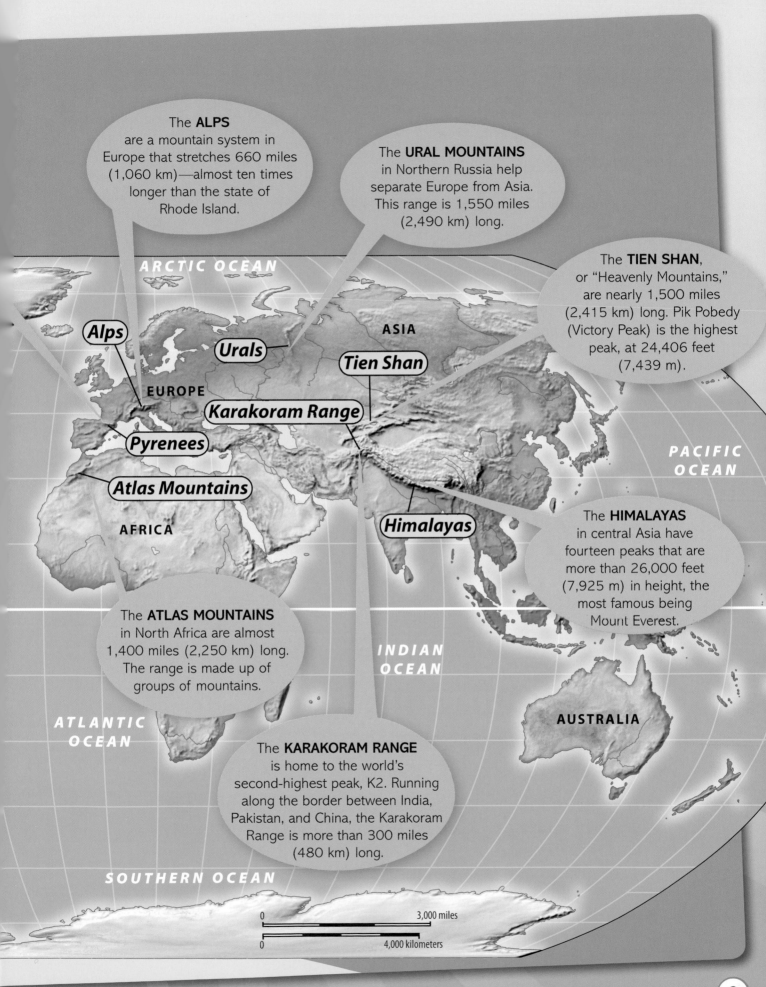

The **ALPS** are a mountain system in Europe that stretches 660 miles (1,060 km)—almost ten times longer than the state of Rhode Island.

The **URAL MOUNTAINS** in Northern Russia help separate Europe from Asia. This range is 1,550 miles (2,490 km) long.

The **TIEN SHAN**, or "Heavenly Mountains," are nearly 1,500 miles (2,415 km) long. Pik Pobedy (Victory Peak) is the highest peak, at 24,406 feet (7,439 m).

The **HIMALAYAS** in central Asia have fourteen peaks that are more than 26,000 feet (7,925 m) in height, the most famous being Mount Everest.

The **ATLAS MOUNTAINS** in North Africa are almost 1,400 miles (2,250 km) long. The range is made up of groups of mountains.

The **KARAKORAM RANGE** is home to the world's second-highest peak, K2. Running along the border between India, Pakistan, and China, the Karakoram Range is more than 300 miles (480 km) long.

ARCTIC OCEAN

Alps

Urals

ASIA

Tien Shan

EUROPE

Karakoram Range

Pyrenees

Atlas Mountains

AFRICA

PACIFIC OCEAN

Himalayas

INDIAN OCEAN

ATLANTIC OCEAN

AUSTRALIA

SOUTHERN OCEAN

0   3,000 miles

0   4,000 kilometers

Map It! How the Rockies Were Born

The Rocky Mountains began forming millions of years ago when two **plates** bumped into each other. This huge collision, which some geologists believe happened about 65 million years ago, pushed the North American plate up, forming the Rockies.

Read It!

Geologic maps show the structure of Earth's crust, such as rock units and fault lines. This map shows Earth's plates and the directions they move in. Each plate is a different color. The arrows show which way the plates are moving. Find the Rocky Mountains on the map. Which plates formed them?

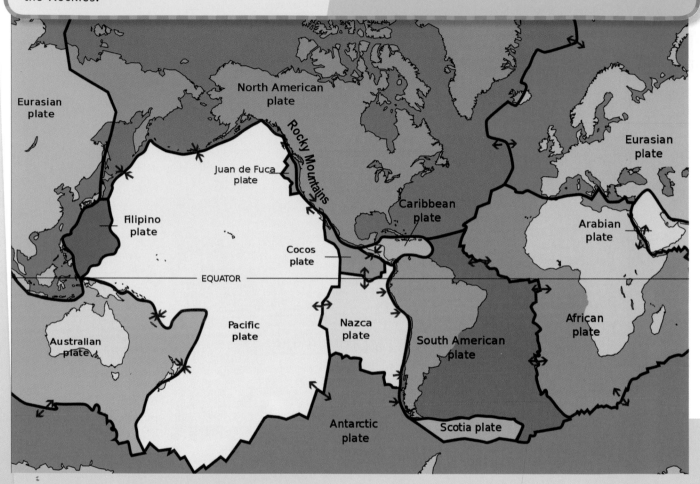

Eurasian plate

North American plate

Rocky Mountains

Juan de Fuca plate

Filipino plate

Cocos plate

EQUATOR

Pacific plate

Nazca plate

Australian plate

Antarctic plate

Caribbean plate

South American plate

Scotia plate

Eurasian plate

Arabian plate

African plate

How Mountains Form

So where did these amazing mountains come from? They all began the same way—with pressure inside Earth.

Earth's crust, or top layer, is made up of huge plates that float on a layer of **molten** rock, called magma. The plates are always moving. Sometimes, when plates crash into each other, rock is forced upward and layers of the Earth's crust fold over one another, creating fold mountains. Earth's crust can also spread and stretch. When this happens, huge rocks slide up and down, forming fault-block mountains. The way magma moves, pools, and cools creates dome mountains and volcanoes.

Activity

Make an Elevation Map

An elevation map uses **contour lines** to show how high a mountain is. The closer the contour lines are on an elevation map, the steeper the land is. Follow the steps to make your own elevation map.

Materials

- clay or putty
- plastic knife
- ruler
- sheet of white paper
- two sharpened pencils
- black marker
- adult helper

1 Mold the clay into the shape of a mountain about 6 inches (15 centimeters) tall. Put it on the sheet of paper.

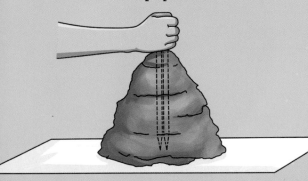

2 Poke the two pencils from the top of your mountain to the bottom. Make sure each pencil makes a mark on the paper. Then remove the pencils.

3 Use the ruler to measure 1 inch (2.5 cm) up from the bottom of your mountain. Mark the spot on the clay with the marker. Repeat this step measuring 2 inches (5 cm), 3 inches (7.5 cm), 4 inches (10 cm), and 5 inches (12.5 cm) from the bottom so that you have marked five sections.

4 Ask your adult helper to cut sideways across each mark until you have five pieces of clay. Remove each piece as you go.

5 Put the bottom piece back on the paper. Line up the holes with the two pencil markings.

6 Trace around the bottom piece of your mountain. Repeat the process with each of the remaining pieces.

7 Label each line with the correct height, or elevation.

And there you have it! Your very own elevation map!

11

Mountains of Fire

It starts with a rumbling deep beneath the Earth. Suddenly smoke and hot **lava** shoot up into the air! A volcano is erupting!

There are more than 1,500 **active** volcanoes in the world—even at the bottom of the ocean. It's important to map them so we know where they are. Scientists also create maps to help them predict where the lava will flow.

Key
- Active volcano

NORTH AMERICA
- Mt. Rainier
- Mt. St. Helens
- Lassen Peak
- Paricutin
- El Chichon
- Popocatepetl
- Coseguina
- Cotopaxi
- Villarrica

SOUTH AMERICA

Pacific Ocean

Atlantic Ocean

Hekla
Surtsey
Helgafell

EUROPE
- Vesuvius
- Vulcano
- Stromboli
- Etna
- Santorini

AFRICA
- Nyamuragira
- Nylragongo
- Kilimanjaro

ASIA

Indian Ocean

- Mt. Fuji
- Unzen
- Mayon
- Pinatubo
- Taal
- Hibok-Hibok
- Krakatau
- Galunggung
- Tambora
- Bam
- Lamington

AUSTRALIA

- Mt. Katmai
- Iliamna
- Mauna Loa
- Kilauea

Pacific Ocean

- Ngauruhoe
- Ruapehu

Mt. Pelee

- Erebus
ANTARCTICA

Map It! Volcano Watch!
It's a challenge, but scientists map all of the world's volcanoes and study their activity. This thematic map shows Earth's most active volcanoes.

Read It!
Look at the map. Which area of the world has the most volcanoes? Which area has the fewest?

How Do Volcanoes Form?

Volcanoes are formed when magma pushes through the cracks in Earth's crust. It rises to the surface where it cools and hardens. More magma builds up on top of that, and a volcano starts to grow.

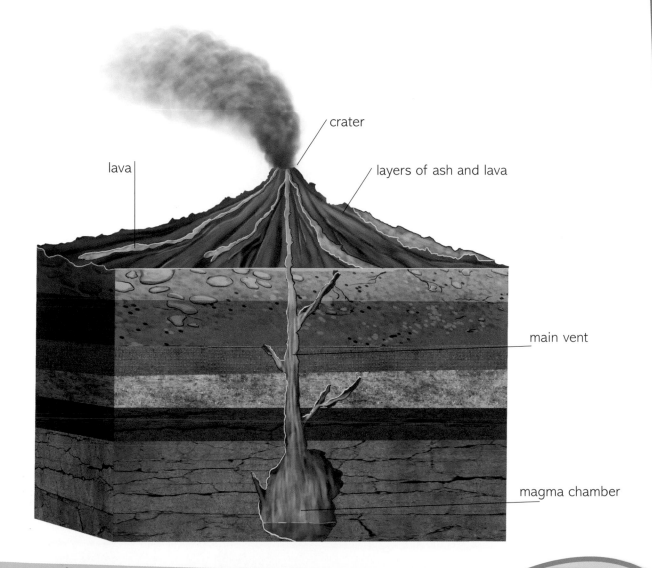

crater

lava

layers of ash and lava

main vent

magma chamber

Why Do They Erupt?

After a volcano forms, magma is still trying to get to the surface. Pressure starts to build up under it. Finally, when the pressure gets too great, the volcano "blows its top," sending lava, gases, ash, and hot rocks shooting up into the air.

Did You Know?

Olympus Mons on Mars is the biggest volcano in the solar system. It's more than 15 miles (24 km) high and 373 miles (600 km) wide!

Mount St. Helens

On May 18, 1980, Mount St. Helens, in Washington State, erupted. Hot ash and gases flew almost 12 miles (19 km) up into the air, and mud poured down the mountain at 90 miles per hour (145 km/h). The eruption caused almost $2 billion in damages! This map shows the area of Skamania County, Washington, that was devastated by the eruption.

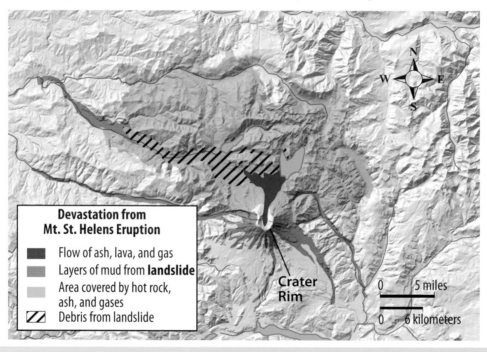

Devastation from Mt. St. Helens Eruption

- Flow of ash, lava, and gas
- Layers of mud from **landslide**
- Area covered by hot rock, ash, and gases
- Debris from landslide

Crater Rim

0 5 miles

0 6 kilometers

Maps in Action: Saving Lives

Can maps save lives? Scientists think they can. That's why they make 3-D maps that show where lava is likely to flow. How? They study the volcano's previous eruptions and use topographical maps to predict how quickly and how far the lava moves. For example, if the volcano is very steep, the lava can travel faster. If there aren't many trees or valleys around the volcano, the lava may go farther. The maps help scientists decide if and when people living near a volcano should be evacuated if it erupts.

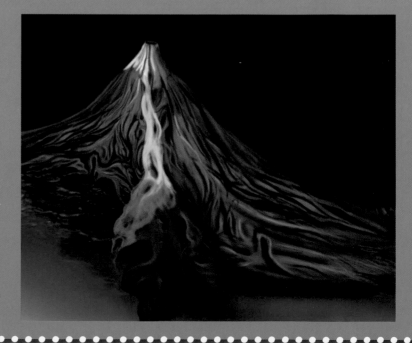

Activity

Mapping Lava Flow

Do you want to see if you can predict lava flow? First, you'll need a volcano!

Materials

- 50-ounce (1.5 liter) plastic bottle
- 2 ounces (60 mL) of water
- 1 tablespoon baking soda
- 1/4 cup vinegar
- 2 tablespoons orange or red food coloring
- 1 piece of cardboard
- 2 feet (62 cm) of chicken wire
- duct tape
- modeling clay or putty
- piece of paper and colored pencils
- newspaper

1 Line your work area with newspaper. Secure the bottle in the middle of the piece of cardboard with duct tape. Make sure the bottle is steady.

2 With an adult's help, cut the chicken wire into a strip about the same height as your bottle.

3 Wrap the wire around the bottle, making a cone shape. Tape the ends together. This is the skeleton of your volcano.

4 Mold the clay over the wire. Try not to bend the wire.

5 Take some more clay and add dips, trails, and ridges. You can also add some trees, buildings, roads, and vehicles.

6 Draw maps of the different sides of your volcano.

7 Predict where you think the lava will flow. Draw the lava flow on your map with a colored pencil.

8 Mix together the water, vinegar, and food coloring. Pour the mixture into the water bottle.

9 Pour the baking soda into the bottle, and stand back!

10 Use a different colored pencil to draw the actual lava flow. Compare your predictions to what actually happened.

nder the Sea

Did you know that there are thousands of mountains underwater? Seamounts and mid-ocean ridges can be found deep beneath the Arctic, Atlantic, Indian, and Pacific oceans.

Up From Below

Underwater mountains are formed when Earth's plates begin to spread apart. As they move, the ocean floor opens up, and steaming hot magma rises up, cools off, and hardens to form rock. More and more magma piles up until finally an underwater mountain is born.

Did You Know?

The Mid-Atlantic Ridge is part of a mountain system that runs underneath several of the world's oceans. This huge system runs for almost 41,000 miles (66,000 km).

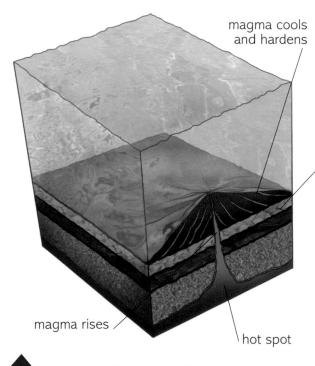

magma cools and hardens

ocean floor

magma rises

hot spot

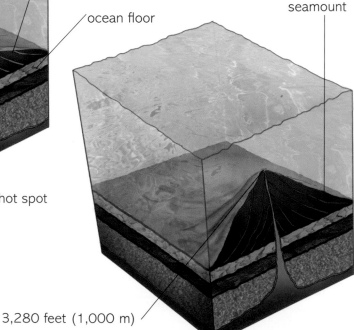

seamount

3,280 feet (1,000 m)

Seamounts are tall—they can rise more than 3,280 feet (1,000 m) above the ocean floor. But they don't rise above the water surface. There are different types of seamounts, but many form over hot spots in Earth's crust, just like volcanoes.

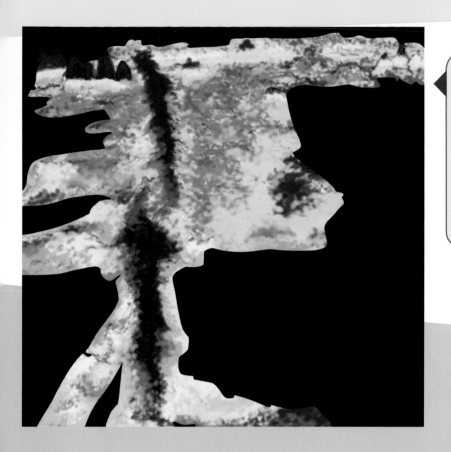

This topographical map shows a part of the mid-ocean ridge in the eastern Pacific Ocean. The brown, red, and yellow areas are above the seafloor. The red areas have the highest elevation. The dark blue areas have the lowest elevation. Notice how the center of the ridge is actually a mountain range.

THE AZORES

The Mid-Atlantic Ridge is one of the biggest undersea mountain ranges in the world. It is about 750 miles (1,200 km) wide and more than 1.6 miles (2.5 km) high. In fact, the Mid-Atlantic Ridge is so tall in some places that it pokes up through the water, creating islands! The Azores Islands are part of the Mid-Atlantic Ridge. These nine small islands all began as underwater volcanoes. They grew over time until their peaks broke through to the ocean surface. Today, almost 250,000 people call the Azores home.

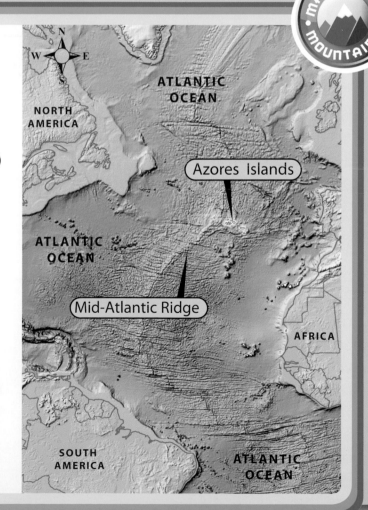

MAGNIFICENT • MOUNTAINS

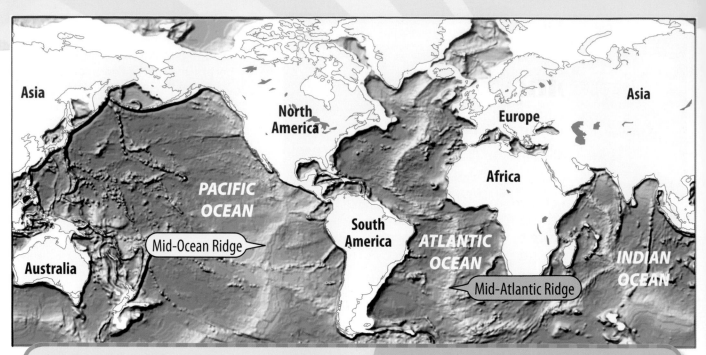

Asia

North America

Asia

Europe

Africa

PACIFIC OCEAN

South America

ATLANTIC OCEAN

Mid-Ocean Ridge

Australia

Mid-Atlantic Ridge

INDIAN OCEAN

Map It! Sea Mountains

It is not easy mapping mountains that are underwater. This map shows the mid-ocean ridges.

Read It!

Follow the path of the Mid-Atlantic Ridge. What shape does it appear to follow? Which continents does it separate?

Breaking Through

How are new islands formed? When an underwater mountain or volcano gets so tall that it rises above the ocean surface. One of the world's newer islands is about 30 miles (50 km) off the coast of Iceland. In 1963 fishers noticed some strange things coming from the ocean—hot ash and rocks were being launched miles into the air. The eruptions continued until 1967. By that time, the volcano had grown so much that the top was above the ocean's surface. Today, the island of Surtsey—named after the Icelandic god of fire—is about one square mile (2.6 km^2). Nobody lives on this tiny island, but scientists are there studying it.

This image shows the volcanic eruptions that formed Surtsey.

Activity

Mapping the Ocean Floor

How challenging is it to map the ocean floor? Try it yourself and find out!

Materials

- shoe box with lid
- putty or modeling clay
- scissors
- 20 drinking straws
- ruler
- marker
- paper
- colored pencils

1 Use the clay to create an ocean floor on the bottom of the shoe box. Be sure to sculpt **plains**, **trenches**, and seamounts!

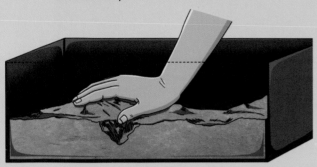

2 Poke twenty pencil-sized holes in the lid of the shoe box. Put the lid on the box.

3 Gently push a drinking straw through each hole. Stop pushing when you feel it touch the clay.

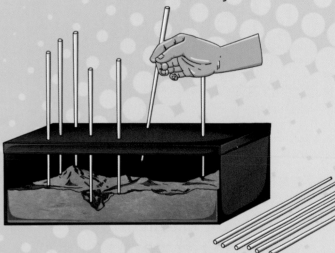

4 Measure the length of the section of the straw sticking out of the shoe box lid. Record each measurement.

5 Using those measurements, create a map of your ocean floor. Label each feature.

6 When you've finished your map, take the top off the shoe box and compare. How well did you do?

Did You Know?

Scientists use the latest technology to map the ocean floor. They use **sonar**, **laser beams**, satellites, and even robots to measure the height of the ocean's features.

Mountain Resources

Mountains provide many of our most important natural resources. We dig deep into mountains for minerals and metals, and we cut down trees for paper and lumber.

What's in There?

Mountains are made of rocks, but what's in those rocks? Often, they contain the metals and minerals we use every day, such as coal, gold, copper, iron, silver, and zinc. Mining can be extremely dangerous for both humans and the environment. Using explosives, as well as complicated machinery and techniques, to mine and dig permanently changes the landscape and can destroy plant and wildlife.

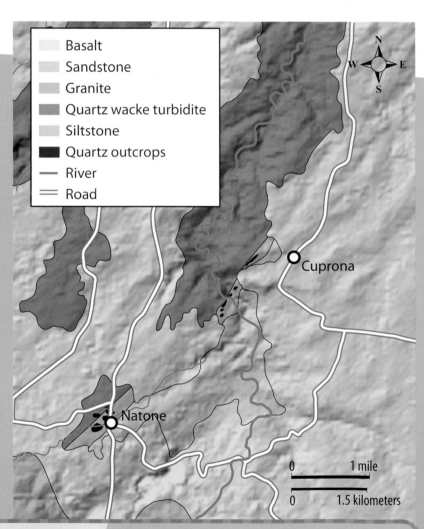

Basalt
Sandstone
Granite
Quartz wacke turbidite
Siltstone
Quartz outcrops
River
Road

Cuprona

Natone

0   1 mile
0   1.5 kilometers

Map It! Mining Mountains

Resource maps show where major mineral **deposits** are located. This map shows the resources around Iron Mountain on the island state of Tasmania, Australia. A large mining operation has begun in this area.

Read It!

Color coding and labels are used to show where the resources are located. Study the map and the key. What minerals are found near the city of Natone?

BINGHAM CANYON MINE

The Oquirrh Mountains, just outside of Salt Lake City, Utah, have been mined for gold, silver, and lead for more than a century. However, these mountains are mainly known for their copper reserves and for the famous Bingham Canyon Mine. The Bingham Canyon Mine has yielded more copper than any other mine in the United States.

Bingham Canyon is a huge **open-pit mine**. It's almost 1 mile (1.6 km) deep and 3 miles (4.8 km) across. It's hard to believe, but 450,000 tons (408,233 metric tons) of material are removed from it every day. It's so big that astronauts can see it from space!

Did You Know?

The peaks of several Appalachian mountains are being blasted off layer by layer to remove the coal within. Those layers are hundreds of millions of years old! Environmentalists are protesting this method of mining.

Up, Over, and Around

How do you get from here to there when mountains are in the way? It's not easy, but people have been pushing their way through and across mountains for thousands of years. Why? To trade goods and settle new lands.

Trading Goods

Silk. Spices. Amber. Every country in the ancient world had something that others wanted. Once merchants realized this, they became determined not to let mountains stop them from making a profit. Before long, traders in China, Africa, India, and the Mediterranean region began creating maps and planning trade routes. Some routes spanned several countries—even continents. They snaked across deserts, through mountains, and over seas.

JOMSON TRAIL
The Jomson Trail in Nepal is part of an ancient trade route between Nepal and Tibet —areas that were once inaccessible because they were divided by mountains. The entire route is 186 miles (300 km) long and winds through the Annapurna Mountain Range in the Himalaya Mountains. Many towns were settled along this route.

Did You Know?

Traders brought more than their goods to other countries. They brought their ideas, cultures, and religions. Traders played a major role in helping nations learn about other places and people.

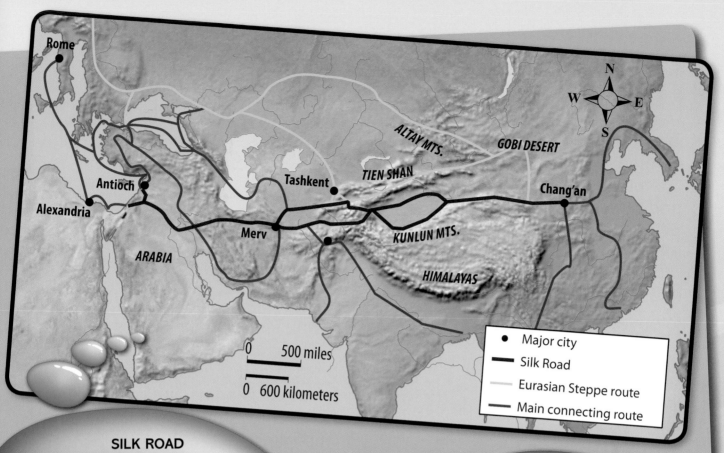

Legend:
- ● Major city
- ▬ Silk Road
- ▬ Eurasian Steppe route
- ▬ Main connecting route

Map labels: Rome, Antioch, Alexandria, ARABIA, Merv, Tashkent, TIEN SHAN, ALTAY MTS., GOBI DESERT, KUNLUN MTS., HIMALAYAS, Chang'an

Scale: 0 — 500 miles / 0 — 600 kilometers

SILK ROAD

One of the earliest trade routes, later known as Silk Road, was 4,000 miles (6,400 km) long! Traders traveled in caravans of more than one hundred camels loaded down with goods such as paper, furs, tea, spices, ivory, and glass. The Chinese finally mapped this route—a task that took years.

OLD SPANISH TRAIL

In 1776 Spanish explorers began searching for a trade route to connect the areas that are now New Mexico and California. The areas were 1,200 miles (1,900 km) apart and were separated by mountains, canyons, and deserts. It took more than fifty years to find a safe route.

Legend:
- ▬ Old Spanish trail
- ═ Modern highways

Map labels: Colorado, Utah, California, Santa Fe, Arizona, New Mexico, Los Angeles

Scale: 0 — 200 miles / 0 — 300 kilometers

Moving On!

Trade was just one reason people wanted to conquer mountains. The other was the urge to explore and settle new lands. Adventurous people risked their lives to find out what was beyond the horizon.

By the end of the 1700s, the western United States was one of the last new frontiers. Thousands of Americans headed west to settle the land. Mountain ranges like the Appalachians made travel dangerous. So explorers and adventurers set off to map safe routes through the mountains.

Daniel Boone discovered the Cumberland Gap through the Appalachian Mountains. Mapping the gap made heading west safer and easier for settlers.

Better Than Wagons

With the invention of the steam-powered locomotive, both trade and travel were transformed. By the mid-1800s, railroad tracks were being laid all around the world.

Laying tracks on flat land is difficult enough, but imagine building them in and through mountains. It was challenging and often deadly! Avalanches, storms, and rockslides were constant threats. Plus, builders didn't have the machinery we do today—tunnels were dug with picks, shovels, and dynamite.

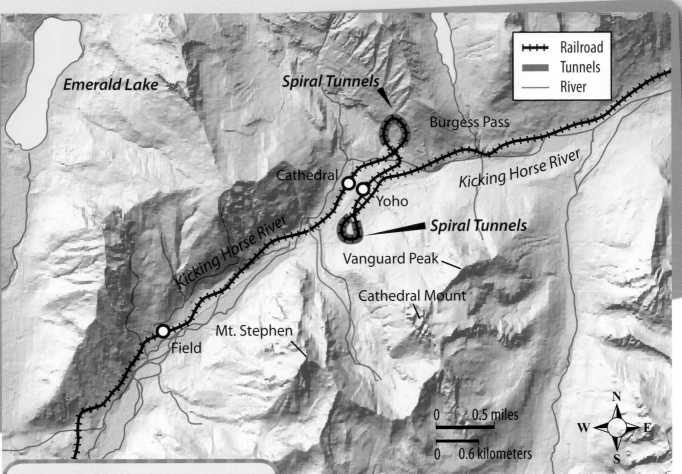

Emerald Lake

Spiral Tunnels

Burgess Pass

Cathedral

Kicking Horse River

Yoho

Spiral Tunnels

Vanguard Peak

Cathedral Mount

Kicking Horse River

Field

Mt. Stephen

	Railroad
	Tunnels
	River

0   0.5 miles

0   0.6 kilometers

N
W   E
S

Map It!
Tunneling Through

In the late 1800s, work began on the Canadian Pacific Railway (CPR), which would eventually connect western Canada with the rest of the country. The tracks had to go through the Selkiri Mountains. Because the mountains are so steep, they built spiral tunnels into the sides of them so the trains could turn and follow the river.

Read It!

Part of the CPR goes through the mountain. The map above shows the railroad tracks, tunnels, and river. Use the scale to figure out how far it is from the northern tunnel to the city of Field.

Work on the Northern Pacific Railway began in 1864. This image shows workers building a tunnel through the Cascade Mountain Range.

Recreation and Adventure

When people look at mountains, they see a challenge. Millions of thrill-seekers flock to mountains every year to hike, climb, white-water raft, and bike. They depend on maps to make sure their adventure doesn't turn deadly.

Avalanches are a concern when skiing. Maps help identify snowy areas that could start to slide.

Serious Fun

What can be more thrilling than swooshing down the slopes? To keep skiers and snowboarders safe on the slopes, resorts carefully map out ski trails. The trails are marked with symbols to indicate the difficulty of the route.

Maps of national parks show routes for hikers, rafters, climbers, or mountain bike riders. Many of these maps also show **nature reserves**—places people aren't allowed. These reserves are created to keep parts of the environment safe from human interference.

Serious Danger

Mountain climbers depend on maps for their survival—knowing where to go can mean the difference between life and death. When you're hanging from a ledge hundreds or thousands of feet in the air, there is no room for error!

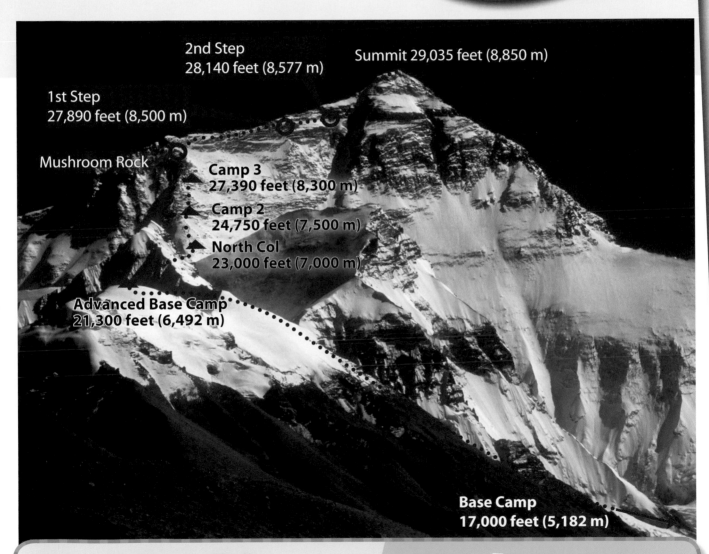

2nd Step
28,140 feet (8,577 m)

Summit 29,035 feet (8,850 m)

1st Step
27,890 feet (8,500 m)

Mushroom Rock

Camp 3
27,390 feet (8,300 m)

Camp 2
24,750 feet (7,500 m)

North Col
23,000 feet (7,000 m)

Advanced Base Camp
21,300 feet (6,492 m)

Base Camp
17,000 feet (5,182 m)

Map It! Going Up!

This map shows the North Ridge route up Mount Everest. The route begins in Tibet. The 1st Step and the 2nd Step are extremely dangerous areas. They mark the final push to the summit.

Read It!

Study the map of Mount Everest. Why do you think Camp 2 and Camp 3 are much closer together than Base Camp and Advanced Base Camp?

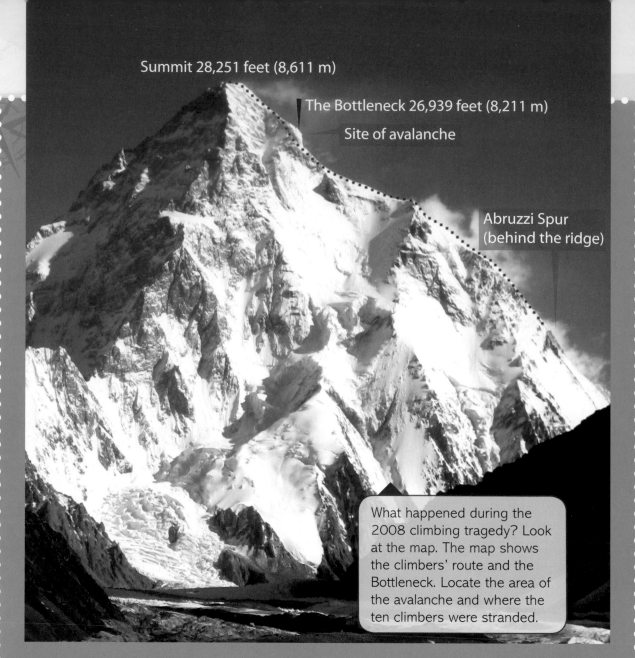

Summit 28,251 feet (8,611 m)

The Bottleneck 26,939 feet (8,211 m)

Site of avalanche

Abruzzi Spur
(behind the ridge)

> What happened during the 2008 climbing tragedy? Look at the map. The map shows the climbers' route and the Bottleneck. Locate the area of the avalanche and where the ten climbers were stranded.

Maps in Action: K2 Expedition

In 2008 a group of twenty climbers made their way up K2. Some of the groups used the Abruzzi Spur route. This route has been painstakingly mapped over the years. Even though it is technically the safest route, it's still dangerous. There are steep climbs, falling rocks, and avalanches.

Eleven climbers in the 2008 expedition did not survive. Two men were killed in the Bottleneck on the way up the mountain. Eighteen people reached the summit. On the way down, a large block of ice fell from an overhang, killing one man and cutting the climbing ropes. Ten people were stranded above the Bottleneck. Some climbers decided to descend in the darkness without fixed ropes. One climber fell to his death, and two died when separate ice blocks hit them. Five more climbers were killed in the fourth avalanche.

Having a map of the Abruzzi Spur route helped rescue teams find and evacuate the survivors. It also helped determine where the bodies of those who died might be.

Majestic Mountains

- Mountains are constantly changing. Over millions of years, all mountains will erode and eventually become soil or sand.

- Avalanches kill dozens of people every year. Falling snow and ice can reach speeds of more than 70 miles per hour (113 km/h)!

- The Jungfrau Railway carries people more than 11,000 feet (3,353 m) up Jungfrau Mountain in Switzerland.

- When Krakatau, a volcano in Indonesia, erupted in 1883, people from more than 2,000 miles (3,200 km) away reported hearing the sound. It was one of the loudest sounds on Earth.

- Glaciers are found in every mountain range except for those in Australia.

- The world's fifty tallest mountains are in Asia. More than 60 percent of Asia is covered by mountains.

Glossary

active A volcano that is erupting or could still erupt.

continents Earth's large landmasses; the seven continents are Asia, Africa, North America, South America, Antarctica, Europe, and Australia.

contour lines Lines that connect points of equal height on a map.

deposits Collections of natural resources.

GIS Geographic information system; used to record and explore Earth's features.

GPS Global positioning system; an electronic navigation tool that uses satellites.

landslide Rock, snow, or dirt falling down the side of a mountain.

laser beams Rays of electric light used for measuring, drilling, and cutting.

lava Hot, liquid rock that rises to Earth's surface.

minerals Natural resources, such as zinc oxide, used to make things.

metals Natural resources, such as gold, used to make things.

molten Melted due to extreme heat.

natural resources Materials and substances found in nature, such as trees, minerals, and fresh water.

nature reserves Protected piece of land, usually for endangered animals.

open-pit mine A mine dug into the earth that is open to the surface.

plains Nearly flat areas of the ocean floor.

plates Huge pieces of Earth that float on top of magma.

satellites Machines that orbit Earth; used for communication and to gather information.

sonar System for finding objects underwater and measuring water's depth by measuring the time it takes for an echo to return from the ocean floor.

summit The very top of a mountain or hill.

trenches Deep canyons on the ocean floor.

To Learn More

Books

Banting, Erin. *Mountains*. New York: Weigl Publishers, Inc., 2007. Easy-to-follow text and engaging photographs bring readers into the world of mountains. Readers learn about the different types of mountains, how they are formed, and the people and animals that live there.

Chambers, Catherine, and Nicholas Lapthorn. *Mapping Earthforms: Mountains*. Mankato, MN: Heinemann Press, 2008. Readers will learn how mountains form and what plants and animals live in mountains. They'll also discover how mountains shape the landscape, people, and the environment.

Webster, Christine. *Mountains*. Mankato, MN: Capstone Press, 2005. Colorful photos and engaging text helps readers explore the world's mountains. Topics include mountain formations, plant and animal life, and people's effect on mountains.

Websites

www.mountain.org/education/
This site offers fun and easy resources for learning about mountains.

www.brainpop.com/science/earthsystem/mountains/preview.weml
Take a closer look at mountains, how they are formed, their environments, and their plant and wildlife.

www.kidsgeo.com/geography-for-kids/0025-usefullness-of-maps.php
See the different uses for maps, map types, and how they are made. This site also includes information about the scientists who use maps.

Index